In the House, Still Light

In the House, Still Light

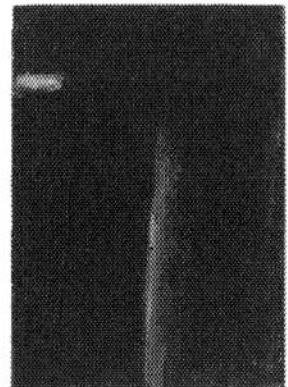

Klaus Merz

Translated by Marc Vincenz

WHITE PINE PRESS / BUFFALO, NEW YORK

White Pine Press
P.O. Box 236
Buffalo, NY 14201
www.whitepine.org

Published in German as *Noch Licht im Haus* by Haymon Verlag, Innsbruck-Wien, 2023

Publication of this book was supported by public funds from the New York State Council on the Arts, with the support of Governor Kathy Hochul and the New York State Legislature, a State Agency and with the support of the Swiss Arts Council Pro Helvetia.

Acknowledgements: See page 109.

Cover Image: Heinz Egger

Printed and bound in the United States of America.

ISBN 978-1-945680-86-1

Library of Congress Control Number: 2024952160

Table of Contents

On Location I

From Hanover

Intermediate State

Voices Nearby

Discerning Paintings

On Location II

Our travail
remains
the task at hand.

I am
working on it,
hands down.

On Location I

The Woman Who Backpedaled

When at last we understood
that even fire hydrants age,
the world around us was already
bursting into flames.

We threw plates and teacups
out of windows and doors,
and we wore warmed linens
rescued from the fiery attic.

"Sodom and Gomorrah,"
a woman whispered,
rooting herself with us
on the sidewalk.

"What is your name?"
we asked.
"I have none,"
said she.

Chess

Between two moves,
the train conductor appears
at the board.

He raises his paddle
and waves us on:
checkmate in Chesterton.

In the House, Still Light

Through the windowpane, I spied
a haggard fellow.
He stood at his bookshelves
as though at his own columbarium:

"Speak, memory, speak!"

Of Travel

I

Staying seated at the table
and waiting until the paintings
leaning on these walls
as accursed witnesses
step out of the frames
of our brief travails
through space and time.

II

My head buried deep in pillows,
I traverse a scenery
not illustrated
on any map:

The coursing rivers
flare up
old scars.

And all the tracks rush down
through the dawn
back to me.

Penitential Hike

Shortly after midnight
the Seven Mountains,
a fragile landscape,
rise ahead toward their heavens.
I climb them barefoot
early in the dawn.

Showers and Storms

These clammy days in July
immerse you
in your ancestor's sweat

(in the evening, across a cooling
countryside, you return home, scythes
draped over your shoulders,
over salt-encrusted, hardened shirts).

And yet, the thunder in your head
remains yesterday's thunder—
a gentle echo of that great
childhood torrent.

Precious Night

New moon; the door
to the past leans open.
Clear images step forth.

A series of fortunate occurrences
rumble for a few moments
under the sternum.

For N.L.

(Grand) Hôtel du Monde

Alone at the dinner table,
and I feel quite tranquil in my own seat.

Across the room, a young woman
offers a breast to her newborn. Also,

the life-force of the remaining guests
continues to evolve.

I shake more salt, then write:

With increasing frequency, this soft
resistance toward everything

that seeks to survey
beyond the situation at hand.

A newspaper still hangs there
on a hook, entirely unread.

Day In, Day Out

The news of the day
steals away the previous
day—and Saharan sand swirls.

And around midnight,
this ravenous lust rises
to snuff oneself out.

Surrounded on All Sides

Watched my neighbor skin
a rabbit from afar.

That bleeding angel stood
as an icon beneath our gilded
childhood sketches. She hangs splayed
behind me on the bookshelf.

Red droplets fall
from that winged apparition,
as if blown to smithereens
through the short green grass.

Heavy bombardment in Kiev,
a radio advises from the kitchen.

Into the Air Currents

For a lifetime he scribbled
the earth beneath
his feet,

but then he laid his pen
aside, and let himself go,
spreading his arms
in free fall.

Keys

To read a heavenly tone
as an organ drone,

improvising
on top

of that hunt
for a voice.

For R.L.

Gentle Stroll

Along the forest's edge,
still traces of snow.
Blackthorn opens

within a cloud
of pollen, and the black kite
pushes off the hazel.

"We only survive death
through dying," my companion says,
pressing ahead through the bramble.

Essay

My attempts at facing
my own internal downward
slope remain unfulfilled.

Even reaching out to Montaigne
doesn't improve my lot: Five hundred

years ago, he suffered from gall-
stones—none helped him carry his pall,
not a single healing word was uttered.

On Location

The cinema of life.
That's a take! The first and
the only one.

The empty director's chair
swivels icily toward
the running camera.

Mythical

Once again
a new morning
thrusts her sharp fingers
between our shoulder blades,
right on the tenderest spot.

From Hanover

Hanover was my home right from the start. Yet, my mother's cooking is the only thing I still practice. How to make more from a little and still be satisfied. Later, came my apprenticeship as a milliner. Is that a job that's still known? As you'll note, I still have this penchant for wearing hats.

A stage and a power outlet is all I need. Tonight it's an Irish pub—they don't have much coin. After I perform, I descend into the cellar, where my host has prepared bedding for me. Tomorrow, I am to go home again, three hundred kilometers, to Hanover-Linden.

Nothing here. No kitchen, no toilet; just a bleak, bare room. It was here I finally found the space to realize my dream of owning a watering hole. For the two of us, there's still no end in sight.

Obviously, we lost a few over the years.

"But actually, we all return," mutters Inga.

After graduation, my plans firmed up. Today, a selection of gourmet coffees stares at me from the coffee table. In my café, it should all be about the experience. No unnecessary components, potted plants, or bric-a-brac—anything that might distract from the actual reason for stopping by.

He reaches for his cup. He wouldn't want his coffee cooled—what with all the talking, and all.

In 1939, we were gifted German nationality. In this fashion, we arrived from the East to Hanover. Even as a young lad, I played the accordion. Word spread far and wide. But, it was my wife who was actually the founder of our music school. Later, in Wettbergen, the everyday still fiddled on. But in 1994, at my pinnacle, I was noodling with the Minsk Philharmonic Orchestra.

Sometimes, I photograph an object before I sketch it. The studio in which I've worked for the past 35 years now sits smack dab in the middle of a hippie commune. Occasionally, we start up a jam. I blow the harmonica, the blues. And every Friday, my son and I have our darts at the ready and our dartboard in view.

I am meditating when I sketch.

I really only set the alarm clock when I have important appointments or meet Mother for breakfast. She loathes tardiness. Otherwise, my day commences around 1 p.m. at the earliest. My best customers are aware of that by now. But if you deliver the good stuff, they'll always be back for more. I pedaled before I was twelve.

The only thing I don't carry in my corner store are groceries—except a few itinerant candies. You can't make money selling groceries. I've known my customers for 30, 40, 50 years; but everything is changing. My newest customers are becoming my oldest.

Also, recently, it has been rather tedious acquiring fresh vegetables.

Already, while I'm walking to the pharmacy, someone slips me a prescription. It has been nearly 60 years since I was born into the apothecary business. I have always tried to approach business with both ethics and economics in mind. Spagyric is my hobbyhorse; *Alchemia vulgaris*, my favorite scent. Lady's mantle helps with most women's health issues.

Unfortunately, I am the last successor.

We offer hydroponics, grief counseling, wedding planning, and grave design—the whole package. For quite a while now, it hasn't been possible to make a living by relying solely on cemetery landscaping. These days, almost half of all burials are anonymous affairs. You don’t want to be a burden to anyone, even after the fact. Death is smothering. As a gardener, that makes me somewhat downcast.

Intermediate State

(1767 / 2022)

I.

Damn this pitiful state: the blindness
of those half-hearted souls.
And the pathetic number who tread
small paths to march in the direction
of truth—far from the deceptions
of that crafty, moribund human self.

II.

So many souls who perish. It seems
a great burden to carry their most important
commandment: *to love.*

Luxuriance, lechery, vested interests,
and vanity are their scurrilous idols. Bah!

III.

Sadly, it's entirely true.
They are deafened
into disregard.
If only a healthy dose of admonishment
swept through their hearts—but
they rouse their ghosts from slumber only
to awaken their own singular prerogative!

IV.

What? Who is waking me up?
I see no one.
Truth or hoax?
Death, hell, a reckoning.
Your sense?
What do these gloomy thoughts portend?

If I had trusted just a handful
of my earlier dreams, it would have
assuaged my constant doubt: Let dreams
remain dreams, I say. But for now,
let us celebrate being awake.

V.

That dreams are just dreams,
I freely concur. But,
it was a voice with a smiting might
that gifted me my peace—which, in a mere
dream, is relatively uncharacteristic.

Still, my limbs tremble.

VI.

There's always another mosquito catcher;
and others, just like himself, barely
permit simple pleasures. That fellow
who shies away from conversation,
with all his hefty moral doctrines,
is rammed full of a fool's naiveté.
His discourse, thoughts, deeds
are simply the peacockery of de-
ception and holy feats.

VII.

Who is that I hear nearby?
Someone here, it seems,
is foraging for approved herbage.
Yes, that is my lot: healing the sick.
I know how to maintain health. Alas,
death is unavoidable, of course:
stay away from icy air—the wet-
afflicted spirit of the times. Trust me!

VIII.

Whoever you may be, keep me
healthy—as once I ever was.
And, should I grow ill, grant me
a full recovery. Lend me your courage and fortitude.
Comfort my slothful soul. And permit me
to understand, serenely.

Voices Nearby

There must be an infinite multitude of cows, if you consider all the milk in the world. I, on the other hand, prefer to guzzle beer. Once, I had unfailingly beautiful teeth. The festering came somewhat later. *Yank!* All of them pulled, both upper and lower. Still, it's better than a toothache, trust me. Eva, another beer! Dear Lord Jesus, accept our gracious hospitality and bless what you have granted us. Recently, the psychologist at work gave me the once-over. "You're quite unwell, my friend," he said. And I spun into a turbulent wind and whirled around the entire workplace.

From the narrow jet bridge, with the cockpit at my back, all the way down to the last five seats: *Equilibrium!* Such are the laws of the air currents. I always perceived my profession as a performance in seriousness, whereby the public becomes increasingly reliant on the invisible laws of life and death. No more discussion. "Tomorrow, I will be indefinitely grounded," my neighbor announces. During the flight home, with my hair standing on end, I surrender to a dying swan.

Weekdays, he floats over the largest construction sites of the region and steers his metal crane. He enjoys looking out along the length of his nose, and spends his lunchtime alone in a breezy cubbyhole. Between the slowly hardening foundations, he can't bear all that complaining and politicizing. Nothing is better than harmony. As temporary timpanist at the county fair, at village parades, and funerals, too, he is still considered the most reliable of the musical ground crew.

The devil only knows why his lad has forsaken him lock, stock, and barrel. "Perhaps he wished I had been somewhat more splendid," he says, and stares over our heads straight at the blank wall.

In the evenings, he follows his son's market predictions and investment tips, just not to lose track. And we, his cohabitants (what a miser he is), stare at the television and, along with him, break into a cold sweat.

I lost my mind, not just out of anywhere. And, since my early childhood, as the daughter of a dedicated animal rights activist, I deeply understand the need for compassion for our fellow man. Doubtlessly for that very reason. But still, questions like these are those that spur me on: Why don't dead birds fall at our feet on a daily basis? Where is their mortuary? And where should I have searched for my activist mother after she revoked herself so early on? In the atmospheres? Or, rather, under a lumbering heap of earth?

I still can't get that large stone out of my head. That very stone my brother Klaus used to take to bed. As a student, I stood awestruck in his tidy hermitage and wrote the word *asceticism* in my school notebook. Later, the menhirs from Yverdon joined us, then Pestalozzi's head too. And our teacher recounted the story of Sisyphus: "Nothing but sanctimonious stones praying for us," she said. "Oppressive and luminous all at the same time."

Even as a child, I navigated the lake at home, counting and watching the ships drift by. Today, I have a legal guardian. He gives me ten francs a day, that penny-pincher. And he's got himself covered five times over.

Slow and steady wins the race. I'm drawing and painting, but I have eaten almost nothing for days. Everything stinks like old cauliflower. Then, I finally wrote the Professor and asked him if he could use a heart. I really wanted to die.

My letter never arrived, thankfully!

And now, finally, I enjoy my life.

What the James Webb telescope captured shows a cluster of five galaxies from the deepest depths of space. The image somehow transports me to the first ultrasounds of our own children: two human galaxies swirling in space. They turn toward us. They drift away from us. And in the darkness that follows, they rise before our eyes as the mischievous reverberations of our own early selves: that strange cluster within the eye of a stroboscope almost going blind in all the glare.

"We know very little about him, virtually nothing at all. No provisional order for a cross, no wreath of roses. Believe it or not, he hadn't even chosen an officiating priest," says the gardener carrying the urn to a communal grave. "The deceased has the same last name as the math teacher in our village. We wouldn't begrudge anyone those two shattered legs more than that fellow. He used to teach us from a camp bed. What could have shattered in the unknown so that he became neither teacher nor gardener, and died entirely abandoned?"

The Wachau turns green. White hotel ships sail their guests to Vienna for the Resurrection. I perch on the shore and bathe a worm on a line. On the newspaper page (which I've chosen to wrap my fresh carp in, rather than read): *Sixty-two year old capsizes in an eddy near the town of Krems.* Fire trucks are deployed around the clock; meanwhile, the ship-breakers are already lounging in dry clothes at their stoves. A young hunter from the village of Mautern rescued the exhausted fellow and brought him back home. Apparently, the two of them toasted Easter together, quite vigorously.

Discerning Paintings

Inside Out

A room, and behind it,
the room remembered.

Between the trees,
the lake loses herself,

and the table laid out
for three guests
juts over the day.

In an alcove, a secret
wobbles intently:

Come closer to the window
and dream what you see.

Continuing the Journey

Desert sails
are hoisted—that is what
I spy: we quietly navigate
into the unknown.

Oasis

Sink a mirror
into the earth, scoop out the water,
and drink with your eyes.

Watercolor

No swell, but in still-
green, a lake.
The painter steals away
on faint feline footsteps.

Return Call

The lichen-dappled trees in this painting
remind me of the flecks of milk crust
snagged in my sleeping
grandson's fiery hair:

Stride fearlessly but quietly
into your enchanted forest!

Beauty

Painted skin, and beneath it
the reason for painting skin.

The woman's contours glow
darkly from within her.

Almost mercilessly, keeping
an eye out, she gracefully burdens
the knowledge of her own beauty.

Busking

Cautiously, on the sidewalk,
the lads cast their first riff.

For two jackhammers,
three shovels, and a pickaxe,

an andante.

Ablaze

This man is ablaze.
He is obliged to rely
on his flint-stone eyes:
the world, wherever
he stares,
is bursting into flames.

Crossing

In Colmar, just like every year,
he ruminates at the Isenheim altar,
to show his reverence
for Matthias Grünewald.
And returning, at the edge of his village,
he paints a tree for Black Friday.

Still Life

In the master's painting,
our underhanded glance
trumps the six of clubs with an ace.
We are still missing the necessary
counter-spell to nail down
this marked deck—
the teapot, the cup, the book.
Ceci n'est pas une pipe.

Over the Water

The mother's countenance
calcifies the child's face.
A picture becomes an inner picture
we soon find ourselves caught within.

What I Saw with Mine Own Eyes

I.

Maria spreads out her cloak.
The blue fabric seeps beneath
the bolted door; it forms
the foundations for life
in this invisible city where
one hand clasps the other, tight.

II.

A woman draws her poetry
from a cloudbank amassing on the shore
and enters within. She feels
her way along her lifelines, the guiding
hand of their flowing currents, which are in-
scripted, and chronicle her inner-most life.

III.

A handcrafted network
of coordinates plots out
our last oyster supper.
Our eyes measure out what has been served up.
Behind, the ocean is tearing up; and thus,
we return home over crags, over reefs—
and, quite conspicuously—over what
can't quite be perceived.

IV.

Right here, scissors snip
at Felix Vallotton's sisters, se-
parating their dark from their light.
We follow that sharp incision
with finger precision—pregnant pos-
sibilites spill on dark ground
all the way to the end—when Judith
arrives with a collection of Swiss army knives:
blades upon blades that reveal a sharper soul.

Marlboro Man

He should have known better.
Smoking is deadly.
It's just the cigarette pack
that still clings
to the fallen rider's saddle.
And the horse, the horse bleeds too.

Low Sun

Stored beneath the awning,
seven siblings' toys.

The plastic doll
of the gentlest little child
casts no shadow.

Solitaire

A woman intends
to play, but is
played. The warmth

rising from her palm comes
as quite a shock. She
almost counts herself

among the shadows;
yet her heart and
her ruby-red lips

might still
save the today.

(Once a) Museum

I

A dress hides
in the fall of its folds.
Three ships
pierce the lake.

From the deployed
cerebral matter
referred to as the retina,
a luminous stimulus
reproduces the next stage.

II

Commander and contour
of self-superimposing
narratives.

The tusk gently
sinks into the
elephant's memory.

III

A hand pulls away
from its own writing. The images
close in upon themselves,

until a blind speck
unmistakably
speaks out.

Evening (Fly to) Spider

You, yes, you with those eight
nimble legs, mosey on over here
and embrace me

before the morning
tears us apart.

Small Wooden Room for I. W.

We drove through the night,
then into the ditch.
We alone, we others,
we third-wheelers.

Felled and lashed tightly together,
magic sprouts rose up
straight out of our rotten
core.

Doppler Effect

He painted walls,
faces, earthly
and heavenly realms—

as well as other
singularities.

On Location II

Intermezzo

Distanced myself
on a three-wheeler
from the wife and family.
My knee joints cracked.

I had always imagined
my entire life
as a false pregnancy;

this, when arrested,
I boasted, was my motive
for fleeing the scene of the crime.

In a Mountain Range

When a cornice of snow awakens,
a young laddie named Lenz
rises out of her warming
snowy gender.

Tides

Waves ebb at the beach,
mussel shells burst open;

and the electroshocks
orally administered by your mother,
years ago, surge

against your own
temporal region.

Laid Out

On the stage,
an open grave;

beside it, a bucket
for moist tissues.

The rest of the evening
unfolds on its own.

Three-Field Crop Rotation

In the beginning was the Word.
Thereafter, that cautious
spelling-out. Then, the reading.
The writing. The hushing.

And between the longing and
the reflection, that tender gray
of a day breaking.

Nuclear Core

Even if he planted himself
in the ring, they would
still say he falters. Also,

daily we seek
that last base camp
for our own demoralization.

Religion

Bring your faith
into safety, advises
my dream devoutly:

That belief in our selves.

Aeon

Twice a day,
between bouts
of eternity,
my stopped
watch displays
the correct time.

Verdict

Now is always.
Never yesterday.
Never tomorrow.
Never ever. And I,
yet another.

Switching Out Road Maps

Nothing exceeds
the punctuality
of our large pickup.

He looms over the house:

"Get in, or spend
your earthly days among
the backpedalers."

Selfie

We turn our backs
to the world, hold
our breaths,

and still can't find
a way out of this chamber
of reverse mirrors.

New Year

Once again I buttoned
myself up incorrectly.

The wind whistles
through an empty slit.

Postscript

Occasionally it hits me
from behind: Take all
those words back.

Translator's Notes and Acknowledgements

In the poem, "Chess," 'Chesterton' replaces the original German 'Trubschachen'. Trubschachen is a municipality of the Canton of Berne in Switzerland, but also functions as a jeu de mots / pun, since the German word for chess is Schach; and the word Trub meaning murky, unclear. For a similar play on words in the English, I settled upon Chesterton–which is a town both in the UK and the US.

In the poem, "Penitential Hike," the Seven Mountains refers to a hill range in the Central Uplands of Baden-Württemberg and North Rhine-Westphalia in modern-day Germany.

In the poem, "Essay," 'Montaigne' refers to the French philosopher of the Renaissance, Michel de Montaigne (1533–1592).

The section "From Hanover" is based on the detailed sociological studies conducted by the students of the Wilfried Köpke High School in Hanover, Germany; the impetus for the series of prose poems came from Kathrin Dittmer of the Literaturhaus Hanover.

"Intermediate State" is an adaptation of the libretto by Ignatz Anton von Weiser for "The Duty of the First Commandment," K. 35, the sacred Singspiel by an eleven-year-old Mozart. In a 'pleasing landscape,' a man lies asleep. The Christian and earthly spirits, Mercy, and Justice, anxiously discuss his predicament. The Wachau, a region in Austria near the Danube, is a popular destination for tourists.

In the prose poem series "Voices Nearby," in the piece that begins "*I still can't get that stone out of my head* … ," Yverdon refers to a Neolithic stone circle (ca. 3,000 BCE) in the town of Yverdon-les-Bain, present-day Canton of Vaud, Switzerland.

"Crossing": the city of Colmar is in the Alsace region of northeastern France. The poem refers to the Isenheim Altarpiece (1512–1516), located in Colmar, which was painted by German artists Nikolaus of Haguenau and Matthias Grünewald. The altar had a significant influence on the depictions of the Nativity of Christ thereafter.

In the poem, "What I Saw with Mine Own Eyes," Felix Vallotton (1865–1925) refers to Franco-Swiss painter and printmaker Félix Édouard Vallotton who was associated with the group of artists known as Les Nabis in Paris.

"Surrounded on All Sides," "Day In, Day Out," "(Grand) Hôtel du Monde," "Of Travel," "Precious Night," and "Gentle Stroll" originally appeared in *The Fortnightly Review*.

"Watercolor" and "(Once a) Museum" originally appeared in *Osiris.*

About the Poet and His Translator

The Poet

Klaus Merz was born in 1945 in Aarau and lives in Unterkulm, Switzerland. He has won many literary awards, including the Hermann Hesse Prize for Literature, Swiss Schiller Foundation Poetry Prize and the Friedrich Hölderlin Prize. In 2024, he won Switzerland's highest literary prize, the Grand Prix for Swiss Literature for his oeuvre of work. Merz has published over 38 works of poetry and fiction. His latest novel is *The Argentinian* and his recent collections of verse are *Unexpected Development* (*Unerwarteter Verlauf,* Haymon, 2013), *What Helios Hauls* (*Helios Transport,* Haymon 2016), *firm* (*firma*, Haymon, 2019), and *In the House, Still Light* (*Nocht Licht im Haus*, Haymon, 2023). In 2022, Merz' selected poems (1963–2016), *An Audible Blue*, translated by Marc Vincenz, was released by White Pine Press, and subsequently won the 2023 Massachusetts Book Prize for Translated Literature.

The Translator

Marc Vincenz is a multi-lingual poet, fiction writer, journalist, translator, editor, musician and artist. He has published over 40 books of poetry, fiction and translation. His recent poetry collections include *The Pearl Diver of Irunmani, A Splash of Cave Paint, The King of Prussia is Drunk on Stars, Thieves' Canto, The Mayfly Codex, Spells for the Wicked, All the Tricks of Language, IRØNCLAD,* and forthcoming in 2026 with White Pine Press, *No More Animal Poems*. His translation of award-winning Swiss poet and novelist, Klaus Merz' selected poems, *An Audible Blue*, won the 2023 Massachusetts Book Award for Translated Literature. He translates from the German, Romanian, French and Spanish. He is publisher and editor of MadHat Press, publisher of the essential journal *New American Writing*, and lives on a farm in Western Massachusetts where there are more spiny-nosed voles, tufted grey-buckle hares and *Amoeba scintilla* than humans.

Also by Klaus Merz in English

Poetry

Out of the Dust
(Spuyten Duyvil, 2015)
Unexpected Development
(White Pine Press, 2018)
An Audible Blue: Selected Poems (1963–2016)
(White Pine Press, 2023)

Fiction

Stigmata of Bliss
(Seagull Books, 2017)
Dreaming Jack
(Spuyten Duyvil, 2025)